*You CA
Dream BIG!
Des The Poet.*

ADOER.

Des the Poet

Tayiah Lewis

You can save lives
Dream Big!
Let the best.

Copyright © 2017 Desmond Earl Bryant White
All rights reserved.
ISBN-13: 978-1974272259

DEDICATION

IN A WORLD FULL OF HATE, SHOW LOVE!

CONTENTS

1. Hashtag
2. Thank You, Trump!
3. Lights
4. Voices
5. Living
6. Time
7. Real Woman
8. Wake Up
9. I Am Moor
10. Walls
11. Dry Rain
12. P.O.M.E.
13. Don't Know
14. Feelings
15. Change
16. One Hundred
17. Respect
18. Emmitt Till
19. Hurricane
20. Love

ADOER.

WE INVITE YOU TO WRITE YOUR THOUGHTS IDEAS DOWN!

BLANK PAGES ARE PROVIDES AFTER EACH PIECE. ROOM TO WRITE ABOUT HOW YOU FEEL. A POTENTIAL START TO YOUR OWN PROJECT. OR EVENTHE NEXT MILLION DOLLAR IDEA.

POST REVIEWS AND COMMENTS TO FIRSTROUNDENT.COM

ADOER.

ADOER.

The time **TO ACTIVATE** is
NOW.

Rise above the madness
And **ELEVATE.**

Hashtag

The oppression, the depression.
Take a second to
appreciate blessings.
When you have it all,
you can lose it all in a second.
I've been tested again I've been tested,
but what was the lesson.
I'm way past regretting.

The time is now,
with no time to be wasted.
I am in denial,
No mirror, I can't face it.
Our reality is that we have made it.
Is it a mirage
or Is it progression

Different shades the same light.
A different day, the same fights.
We see the same stars night,
Like a diamond in the sky.

The same blood in our veins,
The same tears shed when we cry,
The same depth in the ground,
Submerged six feet under

So much death around me
I'm beginning to feel numb.
Where is the love?
I need help!
No GPS, I need help finding some.

ADOER.

In a system built to fail.
What's black on black crime?
When we are killing ourselves.
Its genocide or is it war
Yet still we killing ourselves.
We should save ourselves,
We must save our sons.
People kill people,
Not the gun

Police rather resort to bullets
They shoot bullets
and then off to a resort.
Never thought of using a stun gun
See that would require showing love
of some sort.

Change starts with us,
Hypnotized, confused put in a hex.
A blur, rage, aggression.
Violence, crime, drugs, death and sex.
Our communities are blinded.
Cant you see what's coming next.
When one struggle ends
It's not who's the richest,
When your dead
The money you have wont spend.

Misguided on what is real,
Subconsciously settling for less.
Finding out what is real.
Is finding true happiness.
Its seems we have been misled,
Better yet led astray.
Bamboozled to the truth
There must be a better way.

ADOER.

These times are depressing
and at times can be sad.
I try to keep a smile on my face
Tragedy is becoming a fad.
Killing without retribution
Another body bag, another hashtag.

Where is the love?
A question might I ask?
Just show love when you can
Is that too much to ask?
Is that too hard to do,
It's just too hard to grasp.
Where is the love?
Can it be found in you?
Where is the love?
Look deep inside you.

ADOER.

ADOER.

In these crazy days,
I won't let hatred
decide my fate.

ADOER.

<u>*Thank You, Trump!*</u>

They say a man who does not embarrass
Is a man without a soul?
What's his role?
what are his goals?
What are the true motives?
That is something we may never know.

Is it done for the power?
Is it for the control?
We can't continue to act like we don't know.
Ignorance is bliss,

I've come to appreciate every situation,
That's called enlightenment.
Dude think he's right because
His skin is white,
That's called entitlement.

Thank you trump for exposing those,
The ones on the map
Where the red showed
on the electoral vote.
Where racism is bred,
and bigotry grows.
An eye opener to the anger,
And the oppression that lingers.
My third eye sees danger,
But I'm not here to point fingers.

ADOER.

Make America great again!
I sit back thinking when was it ever great?
I mean it sure wasn't back when
They considered my ancestors as slaves.
It wasn't when they blew up the church
On a beautiful sunny day.
Four innocent girls dead,
All we could do was pray!
Unarmed men killed by the police in the streets,
I see it on the news every other day.
That is not history, it's no mystery.

Make America great again!
I'm not saying that we haven't come a long way.
In 2008 Obama gave us hope,
Made me a believer of change.
It cost to be the boss.
I guess it isn't all about race.
Its more about class,
the wellbeing of your financial state.

Make America great again!
Ronald Reagan created the slogan.
It originated in the 1980s.
The crack epidemic was born
Along with half a million crack babies.

This is the result when you plant seeds
and nurture them with poverty and hatred.
I can't wrap my mind around the thought.
My head is pounding, its aching.
It's filled with frustration.
A nation
confused, yet sophisticated.
A land so beautiful,
Yet history is complicated.

ADOER.

The power is in the mind,
Intelligence and education.
But Donald Trump was our best selection,
No flu shots over here
I have stomach pains, I'm nauseated.
Sea sick with no options
forced in the bottom of a boat.

The pain runs deeper that the ocean.
Consuming leaves that how we cope.
Casted over the edge,
my heart is heavy,
the little cloth I owned is now soaked

The pain runs deeper that the ocean.
The weight on my shoulders
won't allow me to float.
I feel let down, I feel betrayed
A feeling that is not beknown
.
Is this our figure of diplomacy currently?
My apologies if you are offended.
Confused, emotions blended.
It's all love but now I'm serious.

Thank you trump!
What you have done regardless,
Is appreciated and it is relevant.
See now I believe that anyone
No matter how dumb.
Its like anyone can be president.

Even after Obama flawless term,
Trump what you are doing is unprecedent.
You look like the type to judge me guilty
When you don't even have evidence.
You wish to build a wall,
but what is the relevance?
Creating more division
in normal peoples living.
This is what the real question is?

Since you like to put up walls.
Do you support private prisons?
Brick by brick though the lies and the tricks.
We may be too far gone for any human to fix.
America was built on immigration.
And his wife has an accent isn't that ironic.
I can't believe the things that erupts out his mouth
Like a laxative, and it is very toxic!

People put up walls, not to keep people out.
Walls are built to see who cares to break them down.
It's inevitable all walls must someday fall.
If they don't go around, over the top,
They will just go underground.

If you don't fear, that makes you fearless.
If you don't care, that makes you careless.
Even if you comb it over,
I don't care sir,
that still makes you hairless.
I guess trump towers are mirrorless.
The wrongs in themselves people never see.
If I took a stand for my beliefs,
Guess that makes you a terrorist.

ADOER.

Inner city neighborhoods are ground zero,
Where the people there are considered as zero.
What does this mean for the brown and the American negro.
When the president selected sees Hitler as a hero.

Enough power to start a war
Not enough power to bring peace.
Ready to start World War III
Billions of dollars in the budget
But how many people do you help feed?
How many people must bleed.
These are the ones that we won't see.
No more Obama care.
Do we really care?
When we die and there is no money there
we hope that go fund me
has something to share.

Like Hitler he drummed up so much evil and hated.
Promising to once again make America great.
Designed to see how much chaos could be created.
In 2016, not voting may have been my greatest mistake.
In 2020, I'm voting even if its Kanye in the election race.
Not really, I'm joking but could you imagine the debate.
Just saying we are headed for destruction,
If we keep up the pace at this rate.

So, to you mister Donald Trump
I say thank you,
I sincerely want everybody to make it
To get my point across I don't want to fake it.
So, I really want to give all my luck to you!
But for all the ones you disrespected.
Ill end this in all due respect
with a heart felt
Fuck you!

ADOER.

ADOER.

"Where there is no light.
darkness prevails."

Lights

This little light of mine, I'm gone let it shine.
Let it shine, let it shine, I'm gone let it shine.
Its only one problem however,
I can't seem to find mine.
I have a flashlight light on my keychain.
Maybe the batteries aren't in line.
The darker the time,
Is when the light shines brighter.
My thumb is sore,
Constantly trying to spark a lighter.

Anything worth having takes
Patient and time.
To recognize the truth
You must be able to peek through the blinds.
Through these eyes, I have seen a lot.
Although I'm still searching for the light
A path lit by an anointed source.

No coincidence right now,
As I gaze upon a constellation of faces.
You could be anywhere right now
Yet you are here out of all places.
Like a miracle;
The trees, flowers, rivers and the stars,
Gods gospels is in everything
Truth, faith, glory its Gods not ours.
Be grateful for it all,
Thankful for every
day, second, minute and hour.

ADOER.

Its darkness all around,
I don't really know what to do right now.
Its darkness all around,
What would Jesus do right now?

I'm lost, can't seem to find my way.
Don't know which way to go right now.
This little light of mine, I can't find it.
Where would Jesus go if he was me right now.

But what is this, is it a blessing.
I have stumbled upon a path.
Hard times hit us all,
But hard times don't seem to last.

The end is not in sight.
It's down quite some ways,
Struggle, temptation and obstacles
Unfolding lies along the way.
It won't be easy but continue to have faith.

Know that life gets greater later,
Have patience, remember take it day by day.
Open your eyes,
You will see better days.
God shows the proper way.

The deliberate confidence in Gods character
I know I need it in my life drastically.
Faith can move mountains.
"Abracadabra" its majestic, it works magically.

ADOER.

First, we must pray,
One of the hardest thing to do in this days
You can bend your knees to pick up change.
But can't bent your knees to create change.

Trees can grow tall and strong
But everything starting off was once weak.
Just because you gaze upon the height,
Doesn't mean you can look down upon on the seed.

We appreciate the fruit.
Know that the strength is in the root.
We find beauty in what we see,
We trust in the things we do.
Don't ask God to lead your movement,
If you're not willing to willing to move your feet.
The beauty of it is,
That you were not born the form of a tree.

You have the greatest blessing imaginable,
That is the essence of a human being.
Truth is, if you aren't getting efficient light,
It's your job to get to a space you need to be.
A place to where you can receive.
Where you can grow like spring.

Have you ever tried to fly?
But it's like you have brass shackles on your feet.
Wear tragedy as an armor,
Protect me, take me higher
Than my feet could ever take me.
Down the path, I can see the light
And I use the words of Gods to guide me.
Lift the name and give your glory
Watch your soul elevate and grow wings.

ADOER.

I've been searching high and low,
I'm closer than I'll never know.
Blessed with bravery and courage,
So, who would I be not to fight.
Anticipation grows,
Constantly waiting for the right time.

I always felt like something was missing
The diamonds shine on me,
Admiration as they glisten.
Now the light shines from within.
Close your eyes and listen.

Do you hear it?
A voice whispers to me,
I hear it vividly
A conversation clearly,
The voice said,
I know it is a struggle.
And thank you for finding me,
But to keep it real,
between you and me.
It's not hard to find me,
Truth is, you were hiding from me.
The light has always been inside you
.

All you must do is believe.
The devil breaks his back,
Telling lies he tries hard to deceive.
To you I give this light,
Now that you have the best of me.
Know that you are the truth,
and the truth shall set you free.

ADOER.

ADOER.

You will know the Truth by the way it feels.

Trust Your Intuition

Voices

I hear these voices in my head
They are making these voices in my head
Am, I crazy?
Expecting a miracle to come down and save me.
I pray not wish.
I have a God not a genie, it is amazing.
God places everything I need to succeed already inside of me
Tt's free just believe most times we must close our eyes to see.

It's an angel on my right shoulder:
Uplifting me, inspiring me,
Motivating me, never lying to me.
It's the devil on my other,
And he wants to see me fail.
Always wishing me well
He really wants to see me fail.
He wants temptation to prevail.
To see me in bondage, incarcerated,
Trapped behind the glass of a cell.
I don't wish jail on nobody,
On earth it's the closest thing to hell.

When my mind says one thing.
My heart says another.
It was my gut that made the choice.
It was my body that really suffered.
I need my mind, heart, body, soul.
To get along, but they just can't seem to mix
Like water and oil.

ADOER.

Making sounds with my mouth
but my voice sounded muffled.
Over my past obstacle I stumble.
Trying to move forward,
make better choices and progress.

You ever been down and out living without.
It's a hard knock life for us most of us are living it out.
To the point you had to ask yourself, Why me?
What have I done to deserve this?
When you would do anything in the world to overturn this.
Understand this, Ignorance is bliss
You hear a lot but listen to this.

We have been mistaken but now we are awakened.
It took a little shaking but the future is in the making.
With the confidence we are saying, Try me1
I'm not done, I've been through worse than this.

Looking down from above,
Keeping my faith high.
Walking by faith,
Always by my side.
Like a shadow that follows me,
When the sun is setting.
Like a father that guides me
A son of God, blessing on blessing.

Don't let the devil control your body.
Don't let the demons control your mind.
We ignore our inner voice.
That's a God given sign.
Church isn't a museum for good people.
It's a hospital for the broken.
I know a man worth a million dollars
but his soul isn't worth a token.

ADOER.

My circle so small
We could of all fit on a short bus,
Sometimes I be talking to myself
Am I crazy.

Pay it forward,
Give away more than you keep for yourself.
Give unto others as you would give to yourself.
It's not how many followers you have
Hitler had thousands, Jesus only had twelve.

Pray like it's in his hands
Work like it's our own.
When you send prayers up
Blessing come down on.
Sometimes it's not what you want
But it's exactly what you need
It's just disguised as a hidden message.

As I close my eyes,
and I pray with precision.
I'm not perfect
but as I pray I feel my imperfections glisten.
Despite what I'm missing
I'm complete within my soul.
The sacrifices for the goals
And the pain I try to hide.
You don't have a soul
You are a soul,
Respect your body.
Take extra care of the things,
You only get one of in this lifetime.

ADOER.

When God has something in store for you.
He makes life stressful and uncomfortable.
To ensure you must do more,
So always remain gracious and humbled.

Am I crazy, just maybe
But all of yawl are crazy too
You can't judge the next man
Just because they sin differently than you do.
A goal in life is to be honest
And remain true to you
Even if you don't pray for me
I will still pray for you.

ADOER.

ADOER.

Are you living life,
or just paying bill
until you die.

Are you living
or simply existing?

Living

Take a second,
How long is a second?
To thank you for your blessings.
I have had a lot
Then I have lost it all.
Say thank you,
It only takes a second.

I've been tested,
Prepared I've done the work.
Bushes rattle,
Beware that is where haters lurk.
I passed before but when life hit.

I couldn't remember the lesson.
The second guessing.
I blame the oppression,
Why I always received the lesser.

I blame my childhood,
The root of most my depression.
I blame the hunger,
For the times, I got arrested.
I blame society.
Drugs, music the culture digressing.
I try to wake them up,
But they say I am not sleep
my third eye is just resting.

ADOER.

Lives are ending
Meanwhile death is trending.
Food stamp on a paper plate.
We think we lucky and we are
even if sheltered by section eight.
Jails cells filling,
Meanwhile court days are pending.
Tell me how you are living,
I guess orange rompers are appealing.
Don't waive your pretrial
It's just the beginning,

You just may have to sit a while.
Now you are property of the state
Tell me how you are living.
They are balling because they are dealing.
Who's to blame for all the killing.
Kids growing up with no feeling
A hole in their heart
But there is no sealing it.
The pain creates leaks in the soul
But there is no fillings it.
Tell me how are you living.
Change starts with us,
This is just the beginning.

ADOER.

ADOER.

"Time is of the essence. There is no time like the presence."

Time

If you could go back in time
Go back to a younger age.
Would you change the writing on the page?
If you had cheat codes to a new stage.
Does that take the challenge out of the game?
But a win is a win,
so, it may be all the same.

One son, different shades.
One God, different shapes.
What is history?
What if it were all lies.
What is a mystery?
Is it this thing we call life?

Is this the end on my existence when I die?
Life will slip past you
All you can do is ask why.
The light shines down from the sun.
As it radiates life.

Would you walk into the light?
Or would you turn around and run?
There's light at the end of the tunnel
Or am I staring down the barrel of a gun?

Where is the fun?
Love don't seem to last
The last thing most do is fall in love.
The streets don't show love,
The streets aren't cuddled up with no one.

ADOER.

Are you done running the streets
Or caught at the next intersection?
Can't decide if you should hit this liq?
Then hit the mall making selections.
Or go home to your blessings
The aggression and confusion
That is always going through my mind.
If you had on chance,
Would you go back in time?

ADOER.

ADOER.

"A Good Woman
is hard to find
and worth far more
than diamonds."

- Proverbs 31:10

Real Woman

A "bad bitch"
Has nothing compared to a woman on her shit
Confused posting nude hits on the net
Just to get a hit.
To gain a couple likes and comments
On a meaningless pic.
They say they want a gentleman
But to me them actions make me sick.

While caking up making up
Trying to cover it all.
She is photo-shopping the rest
She trying to filter her flaws.
Doing it all,
Just trying to stay involved in the mix.
Thinking her problem is fixed.
Just because she found a new dick.

A real woman on my team,
That's all that i could wish.
Or is it just another love story
To add to my list.
A woman that will ride
From the start to the end.
We can go anywhere girl
Just don't touch my radio once you get in.

An ambitious woman,
With her own belief, dreams and goals.
She inspired me to do better,
I can feel her in my soul.
A real woman is complete,
With confidence and a smile.

ADOER.

Seems like everyone are followers,
So, this should trend for a while.

I want to explore her mind
Before I venture off between her thighs.
Adventurous sex is the best
But behind her eyes is the prize.
She is so humble and doesn't even know it.
She is a blessing in disguise.
Just be honest and sincere
Nothings forever but at least we can try.
We can fulfill those fairy tales,

Like in those books you read and more.
We can go anywhere in the world,
So just be ready for what's in store.
A real man is just waiting
For his eyes to see something real.
Anything less than a real woman
Forces a real man to wait.
I'm just telling you how I feel.

ADOER.

ADOER.

"You cannot wake someone who is pretending to be sleep."

Wake Up

Brothers I don't think yawl understand
The monster in which we are facing.
The life we are living wasn't in God plans
Surround daily by fear, envy and hatred.
It feels like we got over looked
When God handed out his graces.

After almost 500 years of oppression
Enforced on Americas black man.
We are living proof of what society has created.
Where I'm from if you make it to 25,
It's a celebration.
Salute! They say you made it.
The test that were taken
Were received but never graded.

School of the Hard Knox,
Graduated from the streets,
Steal sharpen steel.
This how we were raised to be.
Get wiser as you get older
My heart numbs,
I can't feel. It's unreal.
The betrayal it gets colder.
Tears fall, immediately there frozen.

A chip on my shoulder,
Pain brewing, like a crock pot
Once I pop I can't stop.
Hollow tips dipped in back meat.

ADOER.

The crowed disperse, like a track meet.
All for the love of the cheese
But rats don't deserve to eat.
I mean at least not with me.

Take from the rich and give to the poor.
It appears to us they were born with a little more.
Don't wait for death, to let your wings sore.
A right that your ancestors died and fought for.
The streets don't show no love
How much of your souls is invested?

So many laid down in the streets,
And their soul got infected.
The only cure is love,
But there's no one to send it
They won't show you love
Until your life is ended.

ADOER.

ADOER.

"A people without the knowledge
of their past history,
origin and culture
is like a tree without roots."

- Marcus Garvey

I Am Moor

No one is perfect
Yet everybody tries.
Claiming to be the truth
Yet are full of lies.
Everybody cries,
Just look them in the eyes.

Stay focused on positive,
While cutting all ties.
Clear your mind and focus
On what is real for real.
Don't lose your soul over money
Trying to chase a deal.
Don't lose your life over beef.
He'll throw it on the grill.

Lay it on the line
Expand your mind.
Focus on your grind
Maximize your time.
Do it for yourself,
Stop doing it for the vine.
Take life as it comes
Stay focused on the signs.
Life is a gift,
Acknowledge all your presents
Life is a test,
You got to learn your lesson.

ADOER.

I am Moor,
It shines through my skin, lips and eyes.
I'm educated and, so I've learned
To see through all the lies.
We are more beautiful
Please wake and see.
Anything that we can think
We can make up a way to be.

Somewhere along the lines
We have all been misguided.
Chasing money, cars, clothes
Material objects has us blinded.
When you close your eyes.
Tell me what do you see,
Its Moor black
And it's been that way for all eternity.

If you knew that your ancestors
where all kings and queens.
That means you are Moor
With the potential to be the same thing.
Royalty and loyalty
Stay true to one's self.
How can we be rich?
With no knowledge of self-wealth.

Disregard superficial labels
Given to us by others.
We can create or own images
Such as our black panther brothers.
Mass incarceration
Because they know that we are Moor.
They lie and provide
Miseducation just to keep us on board.

ADOER.

Bound to a way of living
In which they can control.
They know that we are special
Once we set out our own goals.
We become the best
At everything that we do.
We are destined to be Moor
The gift lies within you.
Don't strive for a good job
Create your own destiny.
While doing the unimaginable,
Discovering my destiny.

ADOER.

ADOER.

"You are confined
only by the walls
you build yourself."

Walls

Under my chest,
I feel something pounding.
Banging to escape,
The walls in which I have caged in.
Walls so high,
The most fly can't sore over it.
It was so thick,
An explosive could not penetrate it.

Every day I meditate,
And I urge to set it free.
Although my mind and my heart
Just does not agree.
I believe,
Its afraid of how things may be.
Behind walls it hides,
It hides for its own safety.
Should these walls the opened?

Contemplation which leads to thinking
And thinking leads to drinking.
Realizing it is easy seeking
For the bugs, snakes and rats.
Those unaware to where they were at.
The confused who didn't realize
that the moments where true.
Those who wish to use you
For what you can do.

ADOER.

Given away before but returned
Tarnished and unrepairable.
A brick like feeling in my stomach
Was unbearable it felt terrible.
Glass splitter in my throat
Whenever I swallowed.
The grass is dead on both side,
The death causes sorrow.

It left me empty, hollow.
Eyes filled,
And then something fell.
I kneeled,
Forgive them for what they do not know.
Emotions buried deeply underground.
Sometimes we put up walls
Not to keep people out.
But to see who care enough,
To break them down.

ADOER.

ADOER.

"Keep your faith & always make time to pray."

Dry Rain

Do you see the lights?
Do you hear the thunder bang?
While emotions pour down like
Hurricane rain.
No matter how fast you may run.
You are bound to get wet,
it's an inevitable thing.

Going insane it has left you sulking.
Soaking wet from playing games.
A continuous run in the storm.
Like when you step in the wet spot.
Trying your best not to get your feet wet.

A splash of regret.
Protection from what's next.
Protection from the conditions.
Reflection of my limits
In a puddle that gathers.
A shower can be a relief
Fill the steam and soap lather.

If you get wet by the rain,
It becomes a horrible day.
Sometimes we take life to serious,
Just go outside and play.
Enjoy the stormy weather,
Very few will get the chance.
Next time that it rains,
Just go outside and dance.

ADOER.

ADOER.

"Don't play victim to circumstances you created."

𝓟.𝓞.𝓜.𝓔.

Looking at the windows
Gazing at the stars.
Considering your soul
Wondering who you are.
Contemplating the two
Can't tell which two are closer.
Trying to find the motivation
To do what you're supposed to.

After all the confusion
Tell me what are we supposed to do.
Just grind and be focused
After all that we been through.
If you want to know your past
You should analyze your present status.
If you want to know your future.
Consider your present actions.

Look me in my eyes
Tell me what do you see
Am, I another statistic
Or is there more to me.
Motivated like a soldier
To be all that I can be.
Anything is possible
Making my dreams reality.

ADOER.

Am, I a product of my environment
Or is it a product of me.
I don't make excuses
I just manifest it to be.
Am, I a product of my environment.
Maybe I am
But I believe it brought out the best in me.

When the lights are not turning
And the water not running.
I kept the blinds open,
Just to lets some sun in.
Cracked the windows open.
I was hoping for a breeze
But blessings never came.
Not even when I sneeze.

Praying on my knees,
Times got hard as lumber.
Hunger seems to last longer.
Still I strive to be stronger.
Pondering over my next meal.
I still remember that feeling.
Just trying to make a way out
Without stealing or killing.
Pallets laid out on the floor
On my back,
Looking up at the ceiling.

Eyes closed shut,
Trying to block out the reality I'm seeing.
Then I get to dreaming.
Imaging what I can be then
If wake up put my thoughts into action
Because seeing is believing
People belittle your dreams

ADOER.

Only based off what they can't.
I can't base what I'm gone do
Based off what they ain't.
It's not where you're at now,
But instead its where you're going.
The understood don't need explaining
Sometimes you're better off knowing.

As I grow older
I began to see clearer and realer
How my mom was a user
And my dad was a dealer.
Remembering as a teen
When I pulled my first trigger.
See they robbed me for some change
And in my heart, I had to get him.

But today I thank the lord
Revolver emptied, and I missed him
But another dead body
Or id be lost up in the system
So, we are jumping over fences
Avoiding the consequences.
Taking chances to get ahead
We were neglecting common senses.
Long sentences
It what lies ahead of a corrupted system.

He was innocent but plead guilty
Just so he could keep his freedom.
Going down the wrong path
Because he had no one to lead him
But at some point,
We must do right
And be an example for the children.

ADOER.

See my son will never know
What it's like to be a real nigga
See I figure I can teach him
How to be the bigger man.
How to spend four years in college.
Instead of 48 months in a prison.
How to stay humble and thank God
For the blessing that are given.
My perception

The perception of what the real is has faded
These dudes get gold chains and retro jays
Confidently they will be convinced they made it.
Some black, some white.
Yet so many shades of grey.
Lied by the confusion in which the media portrays.
I try to do something positive.
But I see those who support but are really foes,
Supposedly my bros, friends, relies, homies.
They look at me crazy,
Laugh behind my back, but what is funny?

Something must give,
History repeats its self without changing.
The 80s was a mess,
A true epidemic for the nation.
A poison that destroyed a whole generation.
Mothers 8 month pregnant
Still in the bathroom basing,
Mind wasted.
Father found out he got a junky pregnant.
So, he took off like he was racing,
He couldn't face it.

ADOER.

That same baby 20 years later,
In a jail cell hyperactively pacing.
Thinking, wondering, pondering
About this bid he about to be facing.

Most, people I know struggle.
Obtaining most assets
By the hustle or the muscle.
Living in the world
Where the rich stay rich
And the poor stay poor.
Doing whatever to survive,
Because the tv says sore,
We still need more.

The constant thought of the mind,
Like what am I alive for.
So, robbing, pimping, hustling, slanging, banging.
Are the glorified norms.
The negative life
In which most my brothers where born.
The same reason
Why my generation is torn.
But they say I'm just making excuses.
They must not know this is my reality.

They say America, America, America
The land of the free.
Well nothing has been free at least not for me.
Justice and liberty for all
But I guess that doesn't apply for me.
The more I make the more they take.
If I do wrong, they aren't giving no breaks.
Probation coincidently.

ADOER.

That's only because the plea freed them.
Is this the resignation with freedom?
If you're not in that one percent
There is no way to beat them
Waive bye bye to freedom!
I wish there was a way to gather up
All my mistakes and problems
And just back space and delete them or undo,
But there is not so you reap what you sow.

Experiencing life first hand
That's the only to grow.
We should set our dreams so high
We can't reach them until we are the person
That you need to be.
While surrounding yourself around those
Who want you to be.

Everything that you need to be.
See, we must stand strong and unified
Because together we are a force.
Be grateful for what you have
Because it could always be worse.
One more thing,
Be grateful for everything you have
Because you can't take nothing
With you in a U-Haul
Once you are riding in that Hurst.

ADOER.

ADOER.

"People only know what you tell them."

Don't Know

What they don't know about me
the things I've put behind me.
These are the things that don't show
the nights I put $100 on my "10 or 4"
just rolling always prepared to bet back though.
I've woke up with 0 dollars often
but like a sling shot I always snap back.
I done had many sacks
but I have never sold crack.

Poisoning my own people
see I have never been down with that.
Everybody trying to escape poverty,
so they hit licks, pimping, dealing, stealing and killing,
women stripping for a living
girls twerking for the earnings
but what are they learning.
You say you chasing a bag
but tell me are you losing value
or are your earning?
It's concerning this is a warning.

Can't knock nobody's hustle,
but self-destruction is the ultimate struggle.
Been there, done that
Did my time behind bars
but I'm never going back.
I'm just keeping it real and,
I'm just telling you how I feel and,
if you're as real as you say you are
when you hear this I know you'll listen.

Knowledge is the key.
How you utilize the thought once the doors are open.
I speak these words because tonight the mic is golden
step through to your opportunity
for you may have been chosen!
Just a little about myself you may not be knowing.

ADOER.

"Feelings are just visitors,
Let them come and go."

Feelings

The vibrations of the vibes that surrounds
the fiery passions flaming off the ground
how negativity drowns in emotions so deep,
yet we float like there is no down.
Can you feel it?

Lusting over the small things others may have looked over.
Trusting in things you thought was over.
Dusting places in your soul that hasn't ever been touched.
How the senses go wild off a single touch.

Can you feel it?
If I kiss you gently on your forehead, can you feel it in your toes.
If I sweep you of your feet, can you feel the wind as it blows.
Can you feel it?
I hope it's true, because I can feel it too...

ADOER.

ADOER.

"My only fear is mediocrity."

Change

The things I use to do, I don't do anymore.
For the places I use to frequent I don't go anymore.
I could return to these old places.
But I don't think I live there anymore.

If my keys don't unlock,
Maybe I shouldn't enter those doors.
Same person new eyes
Same guy new times
Old times tell lies
Same lines but I now recognize.

When you are having fun
That's when you lose track of time.
But when you look back and realize
It was a complete waste of time.
All the money in the world,
Could not buy us more time.
If you had all the money in the world
How much time exactly would that buy.

How much would you invest if you could rewind?
At what point would you stop in your life.
First kiss, first love, first time you made love.
Or the biggest mistake in your life
Would you do things different this time?

The time we use to wine
Is time we could use to grind.
Gears turning, levers spinning,
The hands are turning, yearning winning.
Timings wrong, so the time was never right.
If you don't know the time how can you make things right.

ADOER.

A storm came through
so my clock blinks 12:00 through the night.
So, it seems as if my clock has stopped,
Things are steady, but it feels alright.
A clock that has stopped.
If you look at the right time,
At the right time, this time
Will be exactly right.
Time is valuable,
if you spend it wrong you can never get it back.
Enjoying time in the moment that's what most of us lack.

ADOER.

ADOER.

"The average millionaire has 7 sources of income."

One Hundred

I know 100 ways to get $100 in under 100 seconds.
I have never had a plug but always stayed connected.
I received a ton of hate but never affected.
Learning from mistakes made,
Plenty of times been tested
Bob Marley resurrected.
Blow it out, the wish protected.
Rise above the hated
respect is expected.
Too many neglected
it's rough out, its hectic.

If I need my pistol with me,
then I probably should go there.
It's crazy cause then I would go nowhere.
I'm fearless but I'm aware.
From how I look it got them scared.
That's 500 years of oppression,
the condition has them off balance.
Only if you care, take in this wisdom.
Are you u for the challenge.
120 day away, talked the District Attorney
out of a trip to prison.
Public Defended but freedom was the mission.

Better off fending for myself,
Who would listen.
Counting money I'm trying to find myself.
It's when I didn't have a dollar
is when I found myself.
Looking for happiness in this wealth.
Looking for happiness,
its only found in yourself.

ADOER.

ADOER.

"Respect starts with yourself."

Respect

The thought of a bullet burns, internally.
Waiting for the sun to go down
A thief in the night,
An opportunist.
I'm just waiting my turn,
I can't do this.
Negotiating back and forth
Rationalizing my morals,
Anything I have I have earned.

Nothing in life is given
The piercing thoughts,
The penetration
Of information is painful
To think.
My hearts heavy,
She was pregnant
The motion of the ocean
She is feeling woozy
Her mind is spinning.

Like why he chooses me
Like why he uses me
In the ocean
She was casted over
The ride on the slave ship,
For her was no more.
No respect for cargo
No respect for negro.
No respect so I reload

ADOER.

**Respect yourself and regrow
The oppression is suffocating.
If you can't even be yourself.
Everything you thought you were
Turns out your someone else. Know yourself!**

ADOER.

ADOER.

"Our job as parents is to Protect our children. But equally as important is teaching them how to Protect themselves."

Emmitt Till

School days were the best days.
Not a care in sight
even on my worst days
I knew momma would make things right.
Ahead of me are my best days
momma says I'm a star,
so I let my light shine bright.
But even stars die from afar.
Sometimes I miss my father the most at night,
he fought for the country,
but he died in the fight.

It's funny how a life can be ended so abruptly.
So much potential, it's disturbing.
I may not have a lot now
but one day I want to have a lot of money.
If only life were sweet,
the streets were filled with honey,
and no one was hungry,
break bread with those in need
to fill their tummies.
Justice is running, and the streets remain bloody.
My pride is something no one can take from me.
I need to get away.

I'm young but my nerves are bad
I need a new location I need to take a vacation.
I'm on my way to the Money, Mississippi,
where they use a different grammar
the heat down there is scary.

ADOER.

It is nothing out the ordinary
I don't understand the rules down
here the racial lines are very blurry.
What kind of bird is a Jim Crow?
What is freedom I don't know?
All these places they say I can't go.

In the shadows my history hides
slavery was a long time ago.
they say don't play the race card,
Two of everything,
a living duo one for whites
and one for colored folk.
In the south there are a different set of laws,
Many in which to this day we don't know.

Racism is alive and well
with a deadly set of claws.
Oppression weighs us down
if you can't get up try your best to crawl.
I may be young but like a man
I was taught to stand tall
something told me not
to go into the store that day gloomy day.
Never thought I'd be risking it all
Because I had something to say.

ADOER.

I don't know why I felt so daring.
A white woman behind the counter.
I think she caught me staring
She was glaring, thought she was caring
I thought it was a free country.
Things went the other way.

It all happened so fast.
One moment my mom kisses me
I drift off to sleep peacefully.
Bliss turned into a Nightmare
wishing I could change the past
what really happened
no one thought to ask
brutality that is hard to grasp.

I was a kid just trying to nap.
Even though I pray at night
Existing laws that don't make them right.
Tension in the air thickening,
stomach is turning its sickening
legs are weak it's crippling
what state of mind
do you have to be in
To prepare for a lynching?

ADOER.

People yelling,
torches blazing,
tires smoking,
my lungs are choking,
I feel the hatred
I can taste it this is a nightmare
I must be going to jail.

The cross is burning,
I must be going to Hell-o
Jesus what did I do,
what would you do.
Forgive them for they know not what they do.
All this because she didn't know
All this because maybe I don't belong.
the word to my song.
All this but now I am gone

How much does a soul cost?
2 men took mine from me
I didn't think I did anything wrong
I guess I whistled the wrong song
at the wrong time, I just want to go home.

ADOER.

ADOER.

ADOER.

"God doesn't just
send the storms.
He uses them to cleanse us."

Hurricane

Rising when there nothing you can do.
It touches my toes,
like stepping in a wet spot in new socks.
Rising have you ever felt hopeless.
You want to move but
I can't something has my leg
I'm stuck I'm grounded.

Rising to my ankles,
astounded like shackles
I'm bound by no matter
where I go water surrounds.
I just can't seem to shake free.
I try to get away, but
now rising to my knee.

Best used for praying.
As the water rise to my thigh,
I ask why, I ask why. I ask why,
I wait for an answer but no reply.
I ask why do they lie.
I ask why should I try .
I ask why should I rise.
I ask why do I breathe now
it's up to my chest.
Still have faith so still I feel blessed.

ADOER.

I feel like I've been through
worse like I've did more with less.
Yes, I have had it up to here
I hold my head high
Because now it's up to my neck.
Just trying to stay ahead.
Trying to stay afloat
on my tippy toes
trying to see over the horizon.

I see a light now it's binding
eyes to the star,
universe in my eye
passionately it cries, so I cry.
Fashionable late I hold my breath
I'm anxious, like a surprise my hearts racing.

It's rising a young soul lifted higher
a smooth ride to heaven.
To go where anything is possible
to go where everything is probable
where no problem is unsolvable.

So, I Stand
turns out I have been laying down the whole time.
Sometimes you must stand to turn your life around.
Drenched but I'm clean and a step closer to being pure.
No more waiting no more wading by the pool,
No more laying so I stand
but the water is rising.
What do you do,
when there nothing you can do?

ADOER.

ADOER.

"God is Love,
and Love is Real."

LOVE

Love is a four-letter word
along with some more.
Life is a four-letter word
what do you live for.

Live is four letter words
which a lot of us don't do.
Many just live in this world
hoping miracles fall through.

Hope, wish, pray are four letter words
that many of us lean on.
Work hard are four letter words
that we all should depend on.

Know your role as you reach your goal.
Open your mind and expand your soul.
Stretch into who you are and value your cost.
Know your past cause without it you will be lost.

Focused on material gain,
lost in the sauce.
Invest in yourself,
for it cost to be the boss.
A moment of silence
for a soul you've loss.
A short poem that says
Even four-letter words
can get your point across.

ADOER.

ADOER.

ADOER.

SUBMIT A REVIEW INCLUDING YOUR FAVORITE QUOTE, IDEA OR SAYING YOU READ IN ADOER.

ON Firstroundent.com TO WIN A PRIZE

Made in the USA
Columbia, SC
07 May 2018